Art Activities
from the
World of Advertising

DEBI ENGLEBAUGH

1997
TEACHER IDEAS PRESS
A Division of
Libraries Unlimited, Inc.
Englewood, Colorado

To Robert, Taylor, and Morgan

TEACHER IDEAS PRESS
A Division of
Libraries Unlimited, Inc.
P.O. Box 6633
Englewood, CO 80155-6633
1-800-237-6124
www.lu.com/tip

Production Editor: Stephen Haenel
Copy Editor: Louise Tonneson
Proofreader: Kathleen Taylor
Typesetter: Kay Minnis

Library of Congress Cataloging-in-Publication Data

Englebaugh, Debi.
    Art activities from the world of advertising / Debi Englebaugh.
    ix, 145 p. 22x28 cm.
    ISBN 1-56308-451-1
    1. Advertising--Study and teaching (Elementary)--United States.
  2. Commercial art--Study and teaching (Elementary)--United States.
I. Title.
HF5815.U5E54   1997
372.5'2--dc21   97-12082
                                                CIP

Art Activities
from the
World of Advertising

Contents

Chapter 5—ADVERTISING TERMS (*continued*)

Introduction

We are exposed daily to advertisements designed to promote or sell products and services. Advertising is a form of communication used to persuade and influence the viewer through the presentation of information. This book will focus on print media. Words and pictures, the key advertising elements, are explored through a variety of lessons.

Designed as a resource book for teachers with no previous art or advertising experience, this book introduces students to advertising. Lessons are written for younger children, but can be easily adapted for a variety of ages. Minimal supplies are required for teaching the lessons. Easy-to-follow instructions are provided along with reproducible images for convenience.

Chapter 1 serves as a foundation and focuses on the basics of advertising. An introduction to types of advertising, communication, advertising agencies, writing copy, layout preparation, and typefaces are included.

The lessons in chapter 2 explore advertising layout, the arrangement of the art work, copy, and the white space in an ad.

Chapter 3 explores methods students can use to collect information about products and consumers.

Chapter 4 examines various types of advertising media, from billboards to packaging to trading cards.

The lessons in chapter 5 explore advertising terms.

A variety of types of print media are used as the basis for the lessons. Products and services from all aspects of the student's daily life are used as topics for writing. Lessons are designed with a variety of levels of involvement. Some lessons are as simple as creating a brief headline, others require more in-depth writing. The lessons are organized alphabetically by advertising terms.

The lessons are designed so teachers can easily guide students through the processes they are learning. Each lesson includes a brief description, points to remember, a checklist of supplies, and instructions to give students. In addition, most lessons list one or more springboards to related curricular areas. For example, the brochure lesson in chapter 4, in which students create a travel brochure, includes suggestions for geography, history, and literature lessons. There are numerous illustrations throughout the book to use as ad components or as handouts for extended assignments, such as the "Blind Test Questionnaire" in chapter 3.

Chapter 1

Advertising Basics

Advertising is the communication of information about a product or service to potential customers. The information is presented through different types of media that attempt to persuade or influence the viewer.

TYPES OF ADVERTISING

Advertising can be divided into two main categories: institutional advertising and product advertising. Institutional advertising is used to build a company's image and reputation. It is not concerned about an immediate sale. The main goal of product advertising is to sell a product or service.

MEDIA

The method used to deliver the information about a product or service to consumers is called the medium. Different types of media include television, radio, newspapers, and magazines. The lessons in this book explore advertisements from print media such as billboards, brochures, business support materials, catalogs, direct mail, directory advertising, in-store displays, newspaper advertising, magazine advertising, packaging, and posters and signs.

COMMUNICATION

Information must be presented in a way that persuades people. To successfully communicate ideas to potential customers, an advertisement, particularly a product ad, must include the following four main steps.

Attention

Get the viewer's attention. Use an eye-catching headline, including an interesting picture or drawing, or a question to draw the viewer into the ad.

Interest

Hold the viewer's interest. Once you have their attention, show the viewer why it is in their interest to have the product.

Desire

Arouse desire for the product or service. Convince the viewer that the product will meet their needs.

Action

Obtain action from the viewer. Encourage the viewer to buy the product. Provide the necessary information to the viewer so that they can respond: Call this number or complete and mail the order form.

ADVERTISING AGENCY

An advertising agency is a professional firm that handles the advertising needs of its clients. The agency helps the client communicate information to consumers as well as produce the advertisements themselves.

Account Manager

The account manager is the person in charge of an individual company's account. He or she is responsible for coordinating all the people working on an account for a client.

Creative Department

The creative department of an advertising agency produces the ideas for the advertisements. This is where the artists and copy writers work.

Media Department

The media department selects the various media that are appropriate for advertising the product or service.

Research Department

The research department collects and analyzes information that deals with the product or service the company is advertising.

LAYOUT

The layout is the arrangement of the art work, copy, and the white space in an ad. These components of layout can be found on all types of print advertising. (See fig. 1.1.)

Fig. 1.1. Sample layout.

Art Work

The art work in an advertisement can be a handmade or computer-created illustration or a photograph.

Copy

Copy is the text of an advertisement. Ad copy consists of the headlines, body, and captions. Copy is used to inform, persuade, and sell products and services.

White Space

The white space is the empty area around the copy and illustrations. The white space may not actually be the color white; it can be the color of the paper or another background color.

TYPES OF COPY

Advertisements consist of three types of copy: headlines, body copy, and captions.

Headlines

The headline is the large copy in an advertisement that is used to attract the reader's attention. If the headline is not interesting they will probably not bother to read the body copy. Words like *Free, New, Wanted, How to, Improved,* and *Why* are "attention grabbers" and encourage the reader to read the rest of the advertisement.

There are five types of headlines: informative, question, beneficial, target, and action.

1. Informative headlines announce events or provide facts about a product or service, including the product category, product news, and brand or store name.

2. Question headlines arouse curiosity by posing questions.

3. Beneficial headlines give advice and make product claims and promises.

4. Target headlines are aimed at specific customers.

5. Action headlines give the reader specific instructions.

Body Copy

The body copy is the part of the advertisement that communicates information about the product to the consumer. There are two types of copy: factual and narrative. Factual copy states the facts of the product or service, such as its benefits and specific appealing qualities. Narrative copy tells a story about the facts and benefits of a product or service.

Captions

A caption is a brief descriptive sentence usually found under the art work of the advertisement.

WRITING COPY

The following steps may be used as a guide for writing advertising copy. (They are also included as a handout in fig. 1.2.)

1. **Brainstorm Ideas**

   a. Generate a list of ideas about the topic on practice paper, such as the product's positive selling points.

   b. List the type of action the reader is expected to take.

2. **Write the Rough Draft**

   a. Construct the list of ideas into paragraphs.

   b. Because it is a rough draft, there is no need to be concerned with spelling and punctuation.

3. **Proofread and Revise the Rough Draft**

   a. Read the entire rough draft, paying attention to its content, then choose the areas that need more details.

   b. Reread the copy, this time correcting the spelling and checking for proper word usage.

   c. Read the copy one last time.

4. **Produce the Final Copy**

   a. Use the revised rough draft to write a final copy.

EDITING

Grammar, spelling, and punctuation are not a concern in the writing process until the third step. The first two steps, ideas and rough draft, are the creative steps in the process of writing copy. Too much attention to mechanics this early in the process may interrupt creativity. The main purpose of step 3, proofreading and revision, is to improve the quality of the writing. Proofreading marks (fig. 1.3, p. 6) help to make the necessary corrections to the rough draft.

Steps in Writing Advertising Copy

1. Brainstorm Ideas

2. Write the Rough Draft

3. Proofread and Revise the Rough Draft

4. Produce the Final Copy

Fig. 1.2. Guide for writing copy.

Proofreading Marks

℘	Delete	=	Insert hyphen
◡	Close up	⨍	Begin new paragraph
℘	Delete and close up	⎣	Move right
#	Insert space	⎤	Move left
⌄	Insert comma	⎤ ⎣	Center
⌄	Insert apostrophe	∿	Transpose
⌃ ;	Insert semicolon	SP	Spell out
⌃ :	Insert colon	lc	Lowercase
⌄	Insert quotes	cap	Capitalize
⊙	Insert period	stet	Let stand

Fig. 1.3. Editing guide.

TYPE

Type is an important part of the layout's appearance. Typefaces can be divided into two groups: serif and sans serif (fig. 1.4). The small projections coming off the main stroke of the character are called serifs. Sans serif letters have no projections—the lines are uniform. Sans serif is often called block letter type. Serif type is easier to read than sans serif.

Serif

Sans Serif

Fig. 1.4. Sample type.

Type is available in a variety of sizes and is measured vertically in points: twelve point is relatively small, 36 point is large (fig. 1.5).

12 Point New York

36 Point New York

12 Point   Helvetica

36 Point Helvetica

Fig. 1.5. Sample type sizes.

Type can be printed in a variety of styles (fig. 1.6).

New York Normal
New York Bold
New York Italics
New York Outline
New York Shadow

Helvetica Normal
Helvetica Bold
Helvetica Italic
Helvetica Outline
Helvetica Shadow

Fig. 1.6. Sample type styles.

Chapter 2

Advertisement Construction

The lessons in chapter 2 explore the main ingredients
artists and copy writers use to construct advertisements.
The ingredients are arranged to create the advertisement's layout.

DESIGNING AN ADVERTISEMENT

Notes

The questions in figure 2.1 need to be considered when designing an advertisement.

TIPS FOR DRAWING

The following steps are suggestions to assist student drawings.

1. Use practice paper to draw ideas.

2. Always begin with a light pencil sketch. Mistakes are easier to correct if the lines are light.

3. Transfer the drawing to good paper using light lines.

4. Darken the lines to make the final picture.

1. **Reader**
    Who is the target audience?

2. **Positive selling points**
    List all of the good things about the product or service.

3. **Action**
    How do you want the audience to respond when they read the advertisement?

4. **Media**
    What medium or media will be used?

Fig. 2.1. Designing an advertisement guide.

LAYOUT

The layout is the arrangement of three main components in an area. Art work, copy, and white space can be found on all types of advertising.

Toothpaste Advertisement

Cut out and arrange the art work, copy, and white space in the toothpaste advertisement in figure 2.2 to create a variety of magazine layouts.

Points to Remember

1. Keep the layout simple.

2. Viewers usually look at the illustration first.

3. More people read the captions than the body copy.

4. Include the product name in the caption.

5. The headline should be large and bold to capture the reader's attention.

6. Avoid a cluttered layout. Leave sufficient white space to achieve a professional look.

Supplies

☐ Photocopy of figure 2.2

☐ Scissors

☐ Background paper

☐ Glue

Instructions

Make a photocopy of the layout parts in figure 2.2 and cut them apart. Experiment by placing the pieces in a variety of locations on a background paper. Glue the chosen layout to the background paper.

Smile Toothpaste Fights Cavities

Headline

Zero cavities. It's what every parent wants to hear from their children's dentist. Smile Toothpaste has been shown to improve dental checkups when used as directed. Nine out of ten dentists surveyed recommend Smile Toothpaste.

Body Copy

Smile Toothpaste is available in fancy fruit flavor.

Art Work and Caption

Fig. 2.2. Layout activity.

WHITE SPACE

The white space is the empty area around the copy and illustrations. The white space is not always the color white—it is simply the color of the background.

Peanut Butter Label

Use the different-sized headlines, art work, and body copy in figure 2.3 to explore the use of different-sized white space.

Points to Remember

1. A cluttered layout does not appear as professional as one that leaves sufficient white areas.

Supplies

☐ Photocopy of figure 2.3

☐ Background paper

☐ Scissors

☐ Glue

Instructions

Make a photocopy of figure 2.3. Cut out the shapes and place them on background paper. Experiment with the pieces on the background paper. Select a layout that you feel leaves an appropriate amount of white space and glue it to the background paper.

Peanut Butter Peanut Butter Peanut Butter

Contains no preservatives.
Made from only the
freshest peanuts.

Contains no
preservatives.
Made from only the
freshest peanuts.

Contains no
preservatives.
Made from only
the freshest peanuts.

Fig. 2.3. White space activity.

ART WORK

Usually the first thing one sees when looking at an advertisement is the art work: it attracts your attention. If it is interesting, you will go on to read the copy. However, if it is not interesting, you probably will not spend any more time looking at the ad. The art work should help to communicate the advertisement's message.

Newspaper Automobile Advertisement

The art work in an advertisement can be a handmade illustration or a photograph. Use either of these to complete the automobile advertisement in figure 2.4.

Points to Remember

1. One picture is worth a thousand words.

2. Keep the subject of the ad in mind when choosing art work.

3. The art work should arouse the reader's curiosity.

Supplies

☐ Practice paper

☐ Photocopy of figure 2.4

☐ Drawing tools

☐ Old magazines

☐ Scissors

☐ Glue

Instructions

Select the art work to complete the advertisement. If using a photograph, look through old magazines and find an appropriate picture to cut out and glue onto the photocopy of the advertisement. If making an illustration by hand, begin by making several sketches on the practice paper. Transfer the sketch to the photocopy of the advertisement in figure 2.4.

The new family car

Introducing
the New Family Car

Standard tilt steering wheel
Standard air conditioning
Cup holders for all passengers
Standard dual air bags
Up to six-passenger seating

Fig. 2.4. Art work activity.

WRITING BODY COPY

The steps in figure 1.2 are designed to be used as a guide to help the process of writing advertising copy.

Bug Spray Copy

Use the steps in figure 1.2 to help write body copy for the bug spray in figure 2.5.

Points to Remember

1. Write the copy as if speaking personally to the reader.

2. Write as if speaking directly for the client.

3. Use words everyone will understand—everyday language.

Supplies

☐ Photocopy of figure 1.2, page 5 and figure 2.5

☐ Practice paper

☐ Writing tools

Instructions

Write a list of ideas on the practice paper. Create a rough draft of the copy, then proofread and revise the draft. Transfer the completed copy to the photocopy of figure 2.5.

Fig. 2.5. Writing body copy activity.

TYPES OF BODY COPY

Communicating information about a product is the primary purpose of body copy. Factual and narrative are two types of body copy. Factual copy states the facts of the product or service such as their benefits and specific appealing qualities. Narrative copy tells a story about the facts and benefits of a product or service.

Writing Factual Body Copy

Write factual body copy for the vitamins in figure 2.6.

Points to Remember

1. Begin the body copy by relating it to the headline.

2. Give details within the body copy, explaining the benefits stated in the headline.

3. Provide evidence to back up any claims or promises.

4. In the closing paragraph or sentence, ask the reader to take a specific action— to phone, write, mail, or stop in to see for themselves.

5. Write the body copy in everyday language.

6. Include helpful and useful information in the body copy.

7. Make the copy truthful.

Supplies

☐ Photocopy of figure 2.6

☐ Writing tools

☐ Practice paper

Instructions

Write a list of ideas or thoughts about your topic. Create a rough draft of the copy. Proofread and revise the rough draft. Transfer the copy from the practice paper to the photocopy of figure 2.6.

Literature Lesson

Write narrative copy about the vitamins using a nursery rhyme or story.

Fig. 2.6. Factual body copy activity.

WRITING A HEADLINE

Headlines, the largest copy in an advertisement, are used to attract the reader's attention. If the headline is not interesting people will probably not bother to read the body copy. Words like *Free, New, Wanted, How to, Improved,* and *Why* are "attention grabbers" and encourage the reader to read the rest of the advertisement.

Ice Cream Poster Headline

Write a headline for the ice cream in figure 2.7, using an attention-grabbing word.

Points to Remember

1. Creat an eye-catching headline.

2. State the major selling point of the product in the headline.

3. Name the group of people the product or service is expected to attract.

4. Mention the product's name in the headline.

5. Do not put a headline in all capital letters, since it is harder to read capitalized words.

6. Do not place a period after the headline, as it may stop the reader from reading the rest of the advertisement's copy.

7. Do not superimpose a headline over a picture, as it makes the headline difficult to read.

Supplies

☐ Photocopy of figure 2.7

☐ Practice paper

☐ Writing tools

Instructions

Generate a list of ideas about your topic on the practice paper. Write a rough draft of the headline. Proofread and revise the headline. Transfer the headline to the photocopy of figure 2.7.

Available in 55 delicious flavors.
Call 1-800-Ice-Cold for the store near you.

Fig. 2.7. Headline writing activity.

TYPES OF HEADLINES

There are five types of headlines: informative, question, beneficial, target, and action.

Writing Headlines

Write five different types of headlines for a magazine advertisement.

Points to Remember

1. Headlines that announce events or provide facts about a product or service are called informative headlines.

2. Headlines that arouse curiosity by posing questions are called question headlines.

3. Headlines that give advice and make product claims and promises are called beneficial headlines.

4. Headlines aimed at specific customers are called target headlines.

5. Specific directions are given in action headlines.

Supplies

☐ Writing tools

☐ Photocopy of figure 2.8

☐ Practice paper

☐ Old magazines

Instructions

Look through old magazines and select an advertisement. Write a list of ideas about the product or service on the practice paper. Create a rough draft of the five types of headlines. Proofread and revise the headlines. Glue the magazine advertisement to the photocopy of figure 2.8, then, try out each headline by transferring each, one at a time, to the figure.

1.

2.

3.

4.

5.

Fig. 2.8. Headline types activity.

CAPTIONS

The brief description under the artwork in an advertisement is called a caption. Captions are not present in every ad.

Writing Captions

Write a caption for a picture.

Points to Remember

1. Give the facts about the picture when writing a caption.

Supplies

☐ Paper

☐ Writing tools

☐ Practice paper

☐ Old magazines or photographs

Instructions

Select a photograph or picture from a magazine. Cut out and glue the picture to a piece of paper. Look carefully at the art work and write a list of observations about the picture on the practice paper. Use the list to construct a sentence that describes the picture. Proofread and revise the sentence, then write the final copy (caption) under the picture.

TYPE

Type is an important part of a layout's appearance. Type can be divided into two groups: sans serif and serif. Serif type has small projections coming off the main stroke. Sans serif has no projections. Serif type is easier to read than sans serif.

Type is available in a variety of sizes and is measured in points: 12 point is small, 36 point is large. Type can be printed in bold, plain (normal, or roman), and italics.

Examples of Type

Find examples of the different type sizes and styles.

Points to Remember

1. Good typography helps people to read the copy.

2. Do not put a headline in all capital letters, since it is harder to read capitalized words.

3. Do not place a period after the headline. It may stop the reader from reading the rest of the advertisement's copy.

4. Do not use white type on a black background, as it is difficult to read.

5. Do not superimpose a headline over a picture, as it makes the headline difficult to read.

6. Use 12-point type for body copy as it is easy to read—5-point type is too small and 14-point is too large.

Supplies

☐ Old magazines

☐ Scissors

☐ Glue

☐ Photocopy of figure 2.9

Instructions

Look through an old magazine to find the different sizes and styles of type. Cut the letters out and glue them to the photocopy of figure 2.9.

Type Examples

Find examples of different type styles and fonts, and glue them onto this page.

Fig. 2.9. Type examples activity.

LOGOS

Many companies use a symbol that people remember and associate with their product or service; this is called a logo. The logo may consist of letters, pictures, or a combination of the two. The shapes of the letters and pictures are usually simplified, which makes them easy to remember.

Logo Examples

Use old newspapers and magazines to find examples of logos.

Points to Remember

1. A logo conveys identity and a professional look.

Supplies

☐ Scissors

☐ Glue

☐ Old newspapers and magazines

☐ Photocopy of figure 2.10

Instructions

Look through old newspapers and magazines to find examples of logos. Cut out and glue the examples onto a photocopy of figure 2.10.

Logo Examples

Find examples of logos, and glue them onto this page.

Fig. 2.10. Logo examples activity.

Chapter 3

Collecting
Information

Before copy writers can write the copy for an advertisement, they must know as much as possible about the main subject of the advertisement and the people who will see it. The research department of an advertising agency collects and analyzes information about the product or service to be advertised. This chapter will explore methods that can be used to gain such information.

BLIND TEST

A blind test is a method of testing a product by comparing it to a competitor. The results can be useful in planning an advertisement. The test participants are given two different brands of the same type of product and are not told the brand names. They can comment on such aspects as taste, smell, appearance, and texture.

Cookie Taste Test

Set up a taste test in the classroom or at home. Use two different brands of the same kind of cookies. Use a photocopy of figure 3.1 to design a questionnaire for your participants to complete.

Points to Remember

1. Include questions in which the participants use their senses.

Supplies

☐ Practice paper

☐ Photocopy of figure 3.1

☐ Writing tools

☐ Two brands of cookies

Instructions

Select two different brands of the same type of cookies, such as chocolate chip or cream-filled. Write down a list of ideas for questions on the practice paper. Make a rough draft of the questions, then proofread, revise, and transfer the questions to figure 3.1. Use the numbered lines to write the questions. The participants should place their answers for product A and product B on the appropriate lines.

Blind Test Questionnaire

1. _____

   _____

   A. _____   B. _____

2. _____

   _____

   A. _____   B. _____

3. _____

   _____

   A. _____   B. _____

4. _____

   _____

   A. _____   B. _____

5. _____

   _____

   A. _____   B. _____

Fig. 3.1. Blind test.

CUSTOMER SURVEY

A customer survey is a method used to discover a customer's needs or to find out if a customer is satisfied with a product or service.

School Survey

Create a survey for the members of your class to learn their feelings about a school topic, such as lunches, a field trip, a test, or the building.

Points to Remember

1. Keep the survey brief, so the time required to fill it out is minimal.

Supplies

☐ Writing tools

☐ Photocopy of figure 3.2

☐ Practice paper

Instructions

Begin by selecting a topic. Use the practice paper to construct a list of ideas. Make a rough draft of the questions, then proofread, revise, and transfer the questions to figure 3.2. Write the questions on lines 1 through 8. Label columns 1, 2, and 3 with evaluating terms, such as good, fair, and bad.

Fig. 3.2. Customer survey.

INVESTIGATION

Investigation is a method of learning about a product or service. This may be accomplished by looking up information in sources, such as dictionaries, encyclopedias, and various books and magazines.

Museum Advertisement

Use several sources to collect information for a museum advertisement.

Points to Remember

1. Use as many sources as possible to gather information about the museum.

Supplies

☐ Photocopy of figure 3.3

☐ Practice paper

☐ Drawing and writing tools

Instructions

Select a museum to advertise. Use the practice paper to write down ideas and the information you collected. Make a rough draft of the copy, then proofread and revise the copy. Make a sketch that promotes the museum. Transfer the sketch and the final copy to a photocopy of figure 3.3.

Fig. 3.3. Investigation activity.

MARKETING RESEARCH

Marketing research is the collection and analysis of demographics. Demographics are facts about people, such as age, family size, occupation, race, where they live, what they eat, and what they watch on television. A researcher is the person who gathers facts about people. A questionnaire is the research tool used to collect and record facts.

Demographic Questionnaire

Write a questionnaire to discover facts about people.

Points to Remember

1. Determine the general group to be surveyed before writing the questionnaire.

Supplies

☐ Practice paper

☐ Photocopy of figure 3.4

☐ Writing tools

Instructions

Use the practice paper to write down ideas for the questionnaire. Make a rough draft of the questions, then proofread, and revise the copy. Transfer the information to the form in figure 3.4. Use the smaller lines on the right-hand side of the form to record the participants' answers.

Demographic Survey

1. _____

_____   _____

2. _____

_____   _____

3. _____

_____   _____

4. _____

_____   _____

5. _____

_____   _____

6. _____

_____   _____

7. _____

_____   _____

8. _____

_____   _____

Fig. 3.4. Demographic survey.

OBSERVATION

A lot can be learned about a product by using the five senses.

Pretzel Observation

Using sight, smell, hearing, touch, and taste, write a list of observations about a pretzel.

Points to Remember

1.   Use all five senses to discover.

Supplies

☐ Writing tools

☐ Photocopy of figure 3.5

☐ Pretzel

Instructions

Use a photocopy of figure 3.5 to write the observations about the pretzel. Draw a picture of a pretzel in the space above the observations.

Observations

_____

_____

_____

_____

_____

Fig. 3.5. Observation activity.

RECALL TEST

A recall test is used to find out how aware consumers are and how much they remember about an advertisement. An aided recall test asks consumers to recall information directly after they are shown an advertisement. In an unaided test, consumers are not shown the advertisement—they must rely on their memory.

Magazine Ad Recall Test

Using an advertisement from a magazine or newspaper, give an aided recall test to classmates, friends, or family members. Wait a few days, and try an unaided test using the same materials.

Points to Remember

1. Give all of the participants the same amount of time to look at the advertisement.

Supplies

☐ Newspaper or magazines

☐ Scissors

☐ Writing tools

☐ Practice paper

☐ Photocopy of figure 3.6

Instructions

Select an advertisement from a magazine or newspaper. Use the practice paper to take down some ideas, then write a list of questions. Proofread and revise the questions and transfer them to the photocopy of figure 3.6. Show the advertisement to a classmate, friend, or family member. Try both types of recall tests.

Recall Test

Q. _____

_____

A. _____

_____

Q. _____

_____

A. _____

_____

Q. _____

_____

A. _____

_____

Q. _____

_____

A. _____

_____

Fig. 3.6. Recall test.

Chapter 4

Advertising Media

Media is the method advertisers use to send their message to the public. Bulletin boards, billboards, posters, and signs are examples of different types of media. The type of media that is selected for an advertisement depends on the number of people the advertisement needs to reach and how frequently it should be seen.

BILLBOARDS

A billboard is a method of advertising that can be used to create visibility for a company. Billboards are usually placed along high-traffic roads, so that they will reach a large number of people. A billboard's main purpose is not always to make an immediate sale, but to build a company's image. This method of advertising is called institutional advertising.

Billboard for Charity

Design a billboard that advertises a charity.

Points to Remember

1. The advertisement will be viewed from a distance for a short time.

Supplies

☐ Practice paper

☐ Drawing and writing tools

☐ Another paper of any size

Instructions

Begin by selecting a charity for your billboard. Use the practice paper to make a rough draft of the copy and a sketch of the art work. Proofread and revise the copy and art work. Transfer the information to a final paper.

Sample charity billboard.

BROCHURES

Brochures are designed to inform readers about a product or service. A brochure can be a single sheet of folded paper or have a more complex style, which looks like a small book. Brochures can be mailed directly to the potential customer or placed in a display case for easy access.

Brochure for Your Town

A travel brochure is used by vacation areas to attract tourists. The brochure shows the finer elements a place has to offer visitors. The main purpose of the brochure is to make a positive impression on the viewer. Imagine trying to attract tourists to a town. Design a brochure that portrays the community as a town worth visiting.

Points to Remember

1. Use art work on the front of the brochure to attract attention.

2. Include a headline on the front of the brochure.

3. State the main points within the brochure in short paragraphs.

4. Leave room on the brochure for the mailing labels.

Supplies

☐ Practice paper

☐ Writing and drawing tools

☐ Paper for the final design

Instructions

Use the practice paper to write a list of the town's key points. Organize the ideas into a rough draft and make a sketch of the art work. Proofread, revise, and transfer the information to a folded paper, as shown in figure 4.1.

Geography Lesson

Design a country brochure for potential visitors.

History Lesson

Imagine being one of the first settlers in the New World. Design a brochure that will show the attractions of the New World to friends and family back home.

Literature Lesson

Design a brochure for a location in a story.

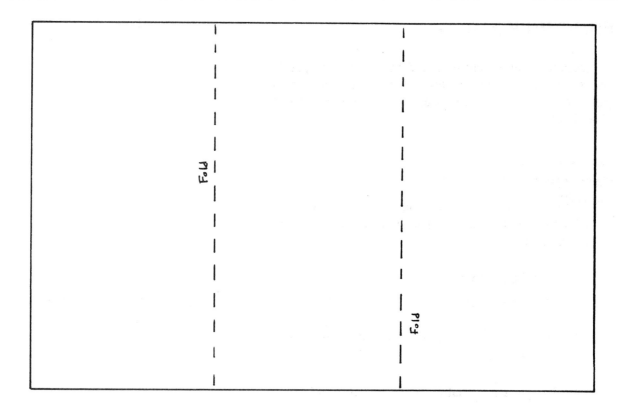

Fig. 4.1. Folding a sample brochure.

BULLETIN BOARDS

Bulletin boards may be found in a variety of public places and can provide visibility for a business. A sign placed on a bulletin board is an inexpensive method of advertising.

Part-Time Job

Design a sign to be placed on a bulletin board that advertises a service that someone provides to earn extra money.

Points to Remember

1. Include art work.

2. Include information about how this person may be reached.

3. Keep the information brief, but informative.

Supplies

☐ Practice paper

☐ Drawing and writing tools

☐ Paper for the final design

Instructions

Write a list of ideas for the sign on the practice paper. Make a rough draft of the copy and art work. Proofread and revise the draft, then transfer the information to another sheet of paper.

Sample bulletin board sign.

BUSINESS SUPPORT MATERIALS

Business support materials are items, such as business cards, stationery, envelopes, invoices, and order forms. They are materials that are used every day to advertise and create a professional image for companies.

Business Cards

Business cards contain important information, such as a person's name, title, business, phone number, and address. Business cards give credibility to a company, making it look established and professional. Design a business card for a particular job.

Points to Remember

1. Include the name of the business and the person's name, title, phone number, address, fax number, and logo.

Supplies

☐ Practice paper

☐ Drawing and writing tools

☐ Photocopy of figure 4.2

Instructions

Select a job. Begin by listing the business card information on the practice paper. Experiment with the placement of the information in the first two blank business cards on the photocopy of figure 4.2. Proofread and revise the rough draft, then transfer the information to the photocopy of figure 4.2.

World History Lesson

During the Middle Ages in Europe, an organization comprised of workers was called a guild. Each guild included members from one type of craft or profession. Design a business card for a guild member from the Middle Ages.

Fig. 4.2. Blank business cards.

Business Stationery

Business stationery is an advertising tool that conveys a company's professional image. Design stationery for a company using a logo.

Points to Remember

1. Include the company name, address, phone number, fax number, and logo.

Supplies

☐ Practice paper

☐ Drawing and writing tools

☐ Paper for the final design

Instructions

Begin by writing a list on the practice paper of all the information to include on the stationery. Make a rough draft on the practice paper of the copy and logo. Proofread and revise the design, then transfer the information from the practice paper to another paper.

Literature Lesson

Use the stationery to write a letter to a character in a story.

World History

Design stationery for a historical figure.

Sample business stationery.

CATALOGS

A catalog is an example of direct mail advertising. Businesses use catalogs as a method of selling their products to potential customers through the mail. Pictures of the products are displayed in the catalog, along with detailed descriptions. The descriptions are very important because the pictures may not accurately show everything the reader needs to know about the product or service.

Writing Copy for Sports Equipment

Write detailed descriptions for the equipment in the sports catalog in figure 4.3.

Points to Remember

1. Give details that let the reader know as much as possible about the product.

Supplies

☐ Photocopy of figure 4.3

☐ Writing tools

☐ Practice paper

Instructions

Observe the items in figure 4.3. If possible, view the actual items pictured. On the practice paper, list the important facts that a customer would need to know about each product. Use the list to construct a rough draft description for each product. Proofread, revise, and transfer the text to the photocopy of figure 4.3.

Science Lesson

Design a catalog for the solar system.

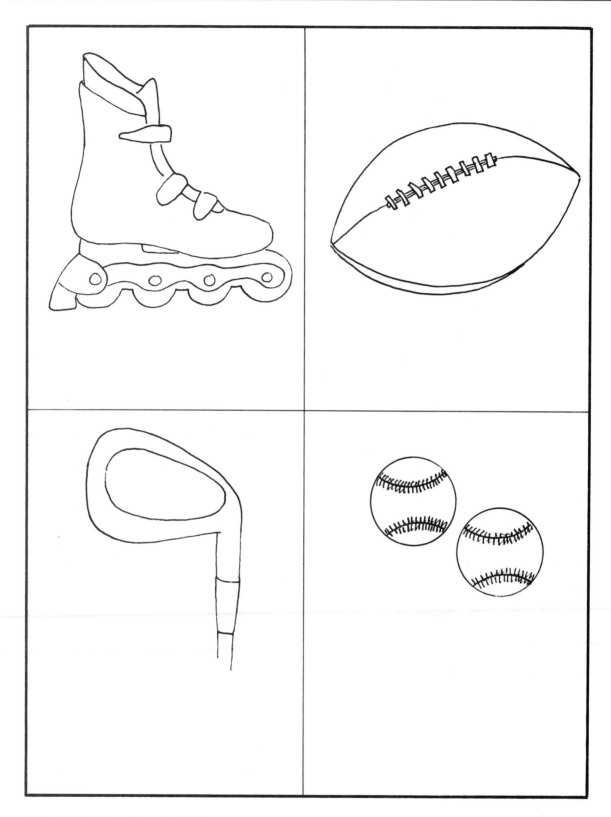

Fig. 4.3. Sports equipment activity.

CLASSIFIED ADVERTISEMENTS

The classified section of a newspaper or magazine is the section used to advertise a variety of goods and services. Classifieds are an inexpensive advertising method and can be written by anyone. For those who want to sell their homes, advertising in the classified section of the newspaper is one method they can use to attract a buyer.

House for Sale

Imagine selling a house, mobile home, or apartment building. Write a classified advertisement describing this home.

Points to Remember

1. Begin with a short headline that attracts the reader's attention.

2. Phrase the facts in short sentences.

Supplies

☐ Practice paper

☐ Paper for the final design

☐ Writing tools

Instructions

Find and read examples of house advertisements from the local newspaper. Take an inventory of a home, and using the practice paper, write a list of all the home's important features. Organize the list into a rough draft. Proofread, revise, and transfer the information to another paper.

Science Lesson

Write an advertisement for a house that is located in outer space.

Group Lesson

Real estate magazines contain a collection of homes for sale in a particular area. This type of magazine is an excellent tool for reaching a specific audience, in this case, people interested in purchasing a home. Write an advertisement for a house that would appear in this magazine. Combine the work from the entire class to create such a magazine.

History Lesson

Visualize how houses looked in the 1800s. Some research on the topic is probably necessary. Write an advertisement for a house of that era that would appear in a classified advertisement.

DIRECT MAIL

Direct mail is a type of advertising that sends information to consumers through the mail. Many people refer to the advertisements they receive in the mail as "junk mail."

Junk Mail Attention-Grabbers

Collect attention-grabbing copy from advertisements that are received in the mail.

Points to Remember

1. Write attention-grabbing copy that makes the reader look at the advertisement.

Supplies

☐ Photocopy of figure 4.4

☐ Glue

☐ Scissors

☐ Junk mail

Instructions

Collect advertisements that arrive in the mail. Use the photocopy of figure 4.4 to display the attention-grabbing copy.

Junk Mail

Fig. 4.4. Direct mail activity.

DIRECTORY ADVERTISING

Directories are a resource to which consumers can refer when looking for a product or service. A directory can consist of one page or can be as large as the yellow pages of the phone book.

Home Directory

Construct a one-page directory of the most popular services a family uses at home.

Points to Remember

1. Include in the directory the company name, address, and phone number and the product or service category.

Supplies

☐ Writing tools

☐ Photocopy of figure 4.5

☐ Practice paper

Instructions

Use the practice paper to construct a list of the services a family uses. Place the services in categories, such as restaurants, groceries, and medical clinics. Create a rough draft of the information. Proofread and revise the copy, then transfer the information to the photocopy of figure 4.5.

Home Directory

Fig. 4.5. Home directory activity.

Yellow Pages Party Supply Shop Advertisement

The yellow pages are a type of directory. When consumers are looking in this directory, they are ready to buy a product or select a service. Design an advertisement for a party supply shop to appear in the yellow pages.

Points to Remember

1. In the advertisement, include the phone number, hours, and location of the business.

2. State the business's specialty.

Supplies

☐ Photocopy of figure 4.6

☐ Practice paper

☐ Drawing and writing tools

Instructions

Using the practice paper, list all of the information to include in the advertisement. Organize the information into a rough draft. Proofread and revise the draft, then transfer the information to the photocopy of figure 4.6.

Fig. 4.6. Party shop advertisement activity.

DOOR HANGERS

Door hangers are a method merchants use to advertise to potential customers in specific areas. Door hangers usually consist of a simple, one-page advertisement that is delivered by hand.

Grocery Store Door Hanger

Design a one-page advertisement for a local grocery store that includes coupons for this week's specials.

Points to Remember

1. Make the store name bold so that it attracts attention.

2. Include the store location and business hours.

3. Include an expiration date on the coupons.

Supplies

☐ Practice paper

☐ Photocopy of figure 4.7

☐ Drawing and writing tools

Instructions

Use the practice paper to write a list of the information to include on the advertisement. Write a rough draft of the copy. Proofread and revise the draft, then transfer the information to the photocopy of figure 4.7.

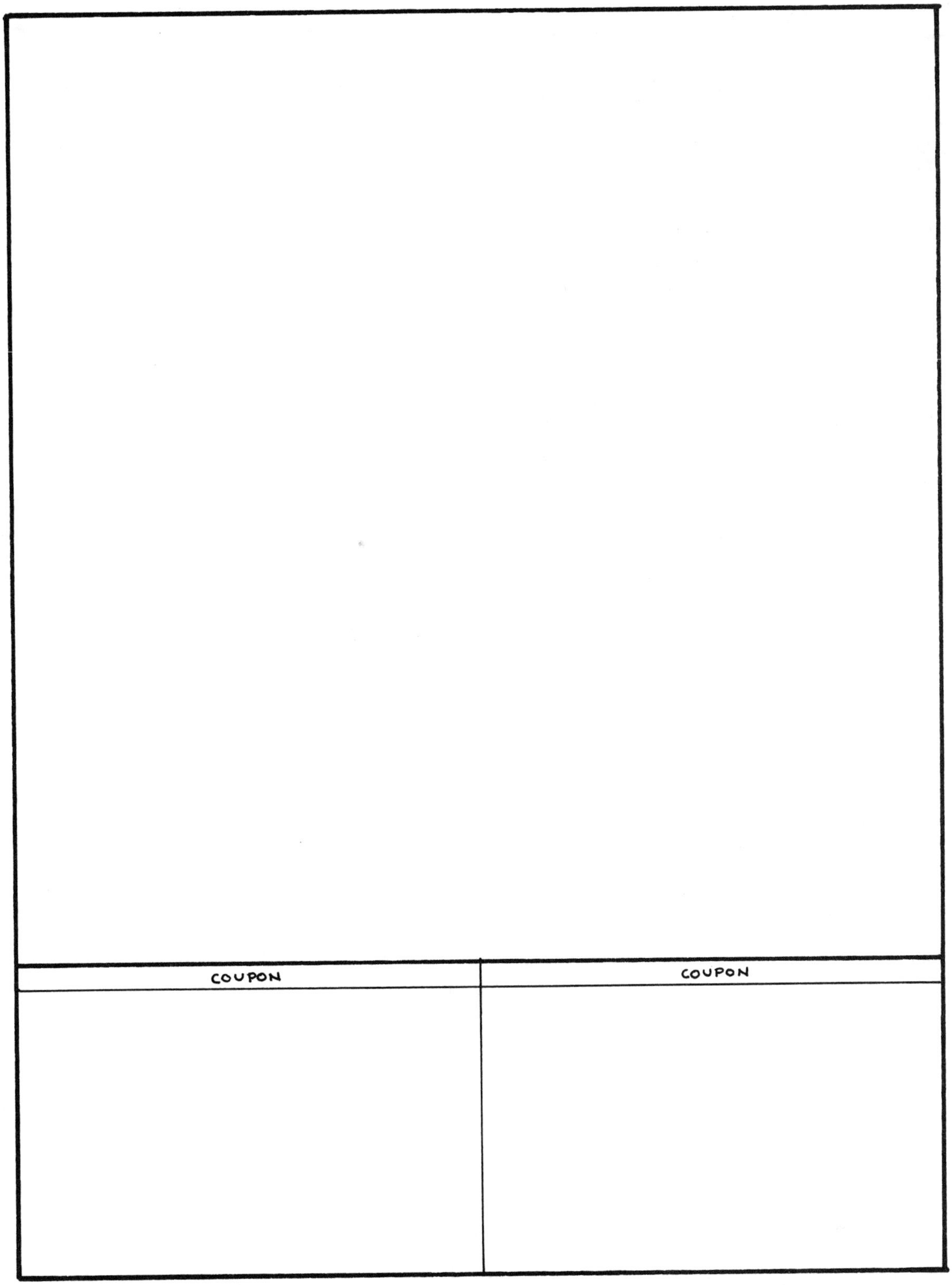

COUPON   COUPON

Fig. 4.7. Door hanger activity.

GIFT CERTIFICATES

Gift certificates are a method of introducing a business to new customers through satisfied customers. Satisfied customers purchase certificates to give others as gifts. Certificates are often sold in $10 increments.

Hair Salon Gift Certificate

Design a gift certificate for a hair salon.

Points to Remember

1. Include the dollar value on the gift certificate.

2. State the name of the business and its location on the gift certificate.

3. Provide a place on the certificate for an authorizing signature.

Supplies

☐ Photocopy of figure 4.8

☐ Practice paper

☐ Writing tools

Instructions

Use the practice paper to write a list of the information you want to include on the gift certificate. Write a rough draft of the information. Proofread and revise the draft, then transfer the information to the photocopy of figure 4.8.

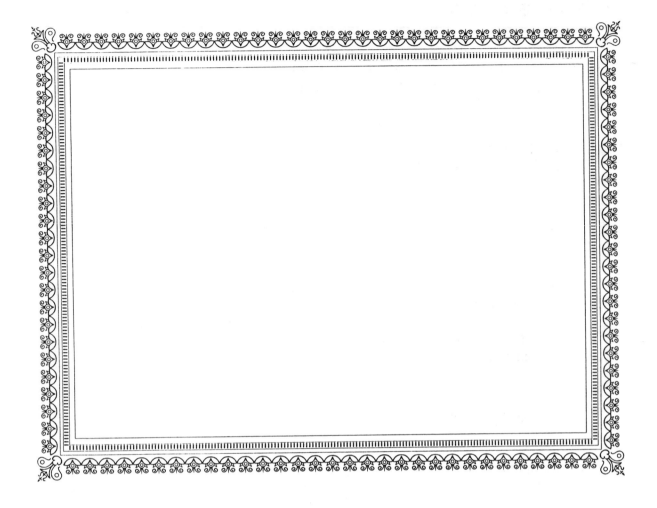

Fig. 4.8. Gift certificate activity.

INSERTS

Inserts are designed to be placed inside of newspapers, magazines, or monthly bills. Inserts that accompany credit card bills, for example, are designed to make it easy for customers to purchase a product or service.

Perfume Insert

Design a perfume insert to send with a monthly department store charge card bill.

Points to Remember

1. Include enough information on the insert to make it easy for the customer to respond to the offer.

Supplies

☐ Drawing and writing tools

☐ Practice paper

☐ Photocopy of figure 4.9

Instructions

Use the practice paper to write a list of the information to include on the insert. Proofread and revise the design, then transfer the information to the photocopy of figure 4.9.

Science Lesson

Experiment with different scents on a piece of paper. Choose a few to send as inserts to promote various products.

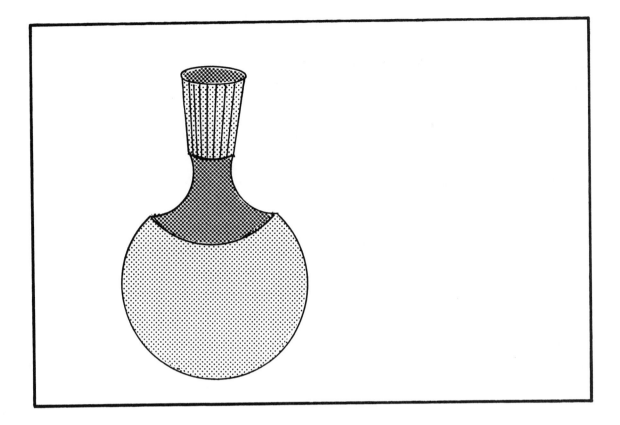

Fig. 4.9. Perfume insert activity.

IN-STORE DISPLAYS

In-store displays, which are also called point of purchase displays, refer to advertising used in a store for products, such as display boxes, racks, signs, and posters. The purpose of the display is to draw attention to a product.

Potato Chip Display Sign

Use the photocopy of figure 4.10 to design a sign for a potato chip in-store display.

Points to Remember

1. Keep the design of the display simple.

2. Use bright colors to attract customers' attention.

Supplies

☐ Photocopy of figure 4.10

☐ Practice paper

☐ Drawing tools

Instructions

Use the practice paper to construct a list of ideas for the display. Make a rough draft of the design. Proofread and revise the rough draft, then transfer it to the photocopy of figure 4.10.

Potato Chips

Fig. 4.10. Display sign activity.

MAGAZINE ADVERTISING

Magazines not only sell advertising space to businesses that are promoting a product, but they must also promote their own publications. Magazines are in competition with each other—there are usually several magazines available on a single topic. The cover must do something to attract readers' interest and encourage them to buy the magazine.

Magazine Cover Design

Design a cover for a science magazine.

Points to Remember

1. Attract the reader's attention by including article titles on the cover.

2. Include eye-catching art work on the cover.

Supplies

☐ Photocopy of figure 4.11

☐ Drawing tools

☐ Practice paper

Instructions

Begin by making a list of ideas for magazine article titles on a sheet of practice paper. Create a rough draft of the titles and the art. Draw the art on a photocopy of figure 4.11. Proofread and revise the copy, then transfer the information to the photocopy.

History Lesson

Select a popular magazine and redesign the cover using a major historical event. Include a date on the cover to convey the time in history to which it refers.

Literature Lesson

Select a popular magazine and redesign the cover using a character from a favorite book.

Fig. 4.11. Magazine cover activity.

NEWSPAPER ADVERTISING

Newspaper advertisements are called display advertisements. Retail businesses can use newspapers to advertise upcoming sales.

Sale Advertisement

Design an advertisement for a local grocery store apple sale.

Points to Remember

1. Use some type of call to action in the advertisement, such as a phone number to call, or a coupon to redeem.

Supplies

☐ Photocopy of figure 4.12

☐ Practice paper

☐ Drawing and writing tools

Instructions

Use the practice paper to construct a list of ideas. Create a rough draft of the body copy and headline. Proofread and revise the copy, then transfer the information to the photocopy of figure 4.12.

Fig. 4.12. Sale advertisement activity.

Newspaper Amusement Park Coupon

Manufacturers and other businesses often include coupons along with their newspaper advertisements. A coupon is a slip of paper that can be used at a business for a reduced rate for a purchase. Design an amusement park coupon that will appear in the newspaper.

Points to Remember

1. Include the coupon value, company name, logo, address, phone number, hours of business, an expiration date, and the days on which the coupon can be used.

Supplies

☐ Practice paper.

☐ Writing and drawing tools

☐ Photocopy of figure 4.13

Instructions

Using the practice paper, list all of the information to include on the coupon. Organize the information into a rough draft. Sketch a logo. Revise and proofread the draft, then transfer the information and drawing to the photocopy of figure 4.13.

Coupon	Expires

Fig. 4.13. Newspaper coupon activity.

PACKAGES

Packages (containers for products) are designed to give products their own identity.

Seed Package

Design a seed package.

Points to Remember

1. Include the name and a picture of the plant on the front of the package.

2. Include step-by-step planting instructions on the back of the package, along with a description of the plant.

Supplies

☐ Photocopy of figure 4.14

☐ Writing and drawing tools

☐ Practice paper

☐ Books for researching the plants

Instructions

Examine several seed packages and choose the elements that are important to include on the package. Select and research a plant. On the practice paper, write down the points to include on the package. Make a rough draft of the copy and art work. Proofread and revise the rough draft, then transfer the information from the practice paper to the photocopy of figure 4.14.

Science Lesson

In order to gain first-hand experience about the plant, perform the actual steps of planting and growing and write about the process from experience.

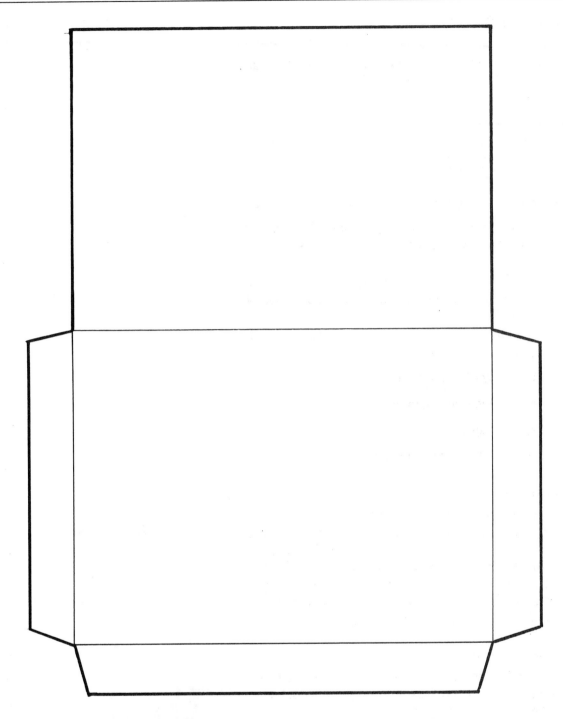

Fig. 4.14. Seed package activity.

POSTERS & SIGNS

Posters and signs are methods of advertising that create visibility for a product or service. Posters and signs are placed in areas that will be viewed by large groups of people.

Campaign Poster

During a political election, candidates rely on posters as one method of attracting the attention of voters. Imagine running for a political office. Design a candidate poster to use in the campaign.

Points to Remember

1. Make the poster's message brief, as the observer usually has only a short amount of time to read the message.

2. Make the letters on the poster easy to read.

3. Design an illustration that will attract a voter's attention.

Supplies

☐ Any size of paper

☐ Writing and drawing tools

☐ Practice paper

Instructions

Select a political office. Write down the key words to place on the poster, along with your candidate's name, the political office, and the desired action for the viewer to take. Make a rough draft. Proofread and revise the rough draft, then transfer the information to the paper for the final poster.

History Lesson

Design a campaign poster for a past presidential election. Photocopy a painting or photograph of a former president, such as George Washington. Place the photocopy and the campaign message on a large sheet of construction paper.

Sample campaign poster.

Theater Poster Design

Theater posters help to describe a featured movie or play. Design a poster for a movie.

Points to Remember

1. Include a drawing or photograph on the poster.

2. Display the name of the movie in large bold letters.

Supplies

☐ Writing and drawing tools.

☐ Any size of paper

☐ Practice paper

Instructions

Select the play or movie to advertise. Use the practice paper to make a sketch and a list of ideas. Organize the ideas into a rough draft. Proofread, revise, and transfer the information and drawing to the final paper.

Literature Lesson

Design a poster for a nursery rhyme or fable that is opening at a theater.

Sign Design

Real estate companies place signs in the front yards of homes that are for sale. These signs attract potential buyers passing by the house. Design a sign that will be used to sell houses for a real estate company.

Points to Remember

1. Make the message succinct, because the observer usually has only a short amount of time to read the sign.

2. Make the letters easy to read.

3. Include the words *for sale* as well as the real estate company's name, logo, phone number, and agent's name.

Supplies

☐ Writing and drawing tools

☐ Photocopy of figure 4.15

☐ Practice paper

Instructions

Use the practice paper to write a list of the information to include on the sign. Draw a sketch of the logo. Proofread and revise the copy, then transfer the information and drawing to the photocopy of figure 4.15.

Fig. 4.15. Real estate sign activity.

Radio Station Transit Sign

Transit signs appear on vehicles, such as buses, taxis, and subways. Design a transit sign for a bus that advertises a local radio station.

Points to Remember

1. Keep the design for the transit sign simple.

2. Include art work on the sign.

Supplies

☐ Writing and drawing tools

☐ Practice paper

☐ Paper for the final design

Instructions

Use the practice paper to write a list of the information to appear on the sign. Draw a sketch of the art. Organize the ideas into a rough draft. Proofread and revise the draft, then transfer the completed information and drawing to the final paper.

Sample transit sign.

Zoo Sign

Design a sign for a zoo using the photocopy of figure 4.16. Include on the sign an illustration of an animal and the name of the zoo.

Points to Remember

1. Keep the illustration of the animal depicted on the sign simple.

Supplies

☐ Writing and drawing tools

☐ Photocopy of figure 4.16

☐ Practice paper

Instructions

Sketch ideas for the animal illustration and the name of the zoo on the practice paper. Create a rough draft, proofread, and revise the sketch. Transfer the drawing and zoo name to the photocopy of figure 4.16.

Fig. 4.16. Zoo sign activity.

POSTCARDS

Postcards are a method of advertising that towns, for example, use to attract tourists.

Town Postcard

Design a postcard to promote a particular town.

Points to Remember

1. Use a picture on the front of the postcard.

2. Include a description of the picture shown on the postcard.

3. Leave room on the postcard for a stamp, address, and greeting.

Supplies

☐ Photocopy of figure 4.17

☐ Practice paper

☐ Drawing and writing tools

Instructions

Use the practice paper to make a sketch of the town. List the town's positive features. Proofread and revise the drawing and copy, then transfer the completed information to the photocopy of figure 4.17. Use one rectangular space on the photocopy for the front, and the other for the back of the postcard.

Geography Lesson

Research a city, state, or country, and design a postcard to promote the area.

Science Lesson

Design a postcard for another planet.

English Lesson

Learn the proper procedure for writing addresses. Use a heavier material, such as oak tag, to construct the postcard, then send it through the mail.

History Lesson

Design a postcard sent by a famous explorer describing his discoveries in a new land.

Fig. 4.17. Postcard activity.

SAMPLE PACKAGES

A method companies use to introduce new products to consumers is to mail out samples. Included in these packages are a coupon and a small portion of the product.

Breakfast Cereal Package

Design a sample package and coupon for a new breakfast cereal.

Points to Remember

1. Include words on the packages like *innovative*, *new,* or *introducing*.

Supplies

☐ Photocopy of figure 4.18

☐ Drawing and writing tools

☐ Practice paper

☐ Glue

☐ Scissors

Instructions

Use the practice paper to make a list of the information to appear on the package and coupon. Make a rough draft of both. Sketch the cereal box art. Proofread and revise the rough draft, then transfer the information and drawing to the photocopy of figure 4.18. Cut, fold, and glue the photocopy to form the cereal box.

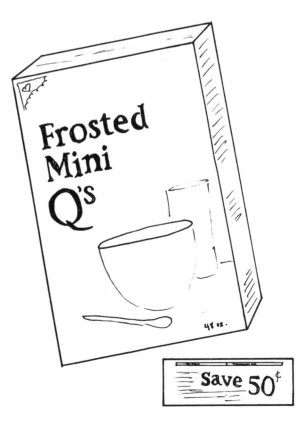

Sample cereal package.

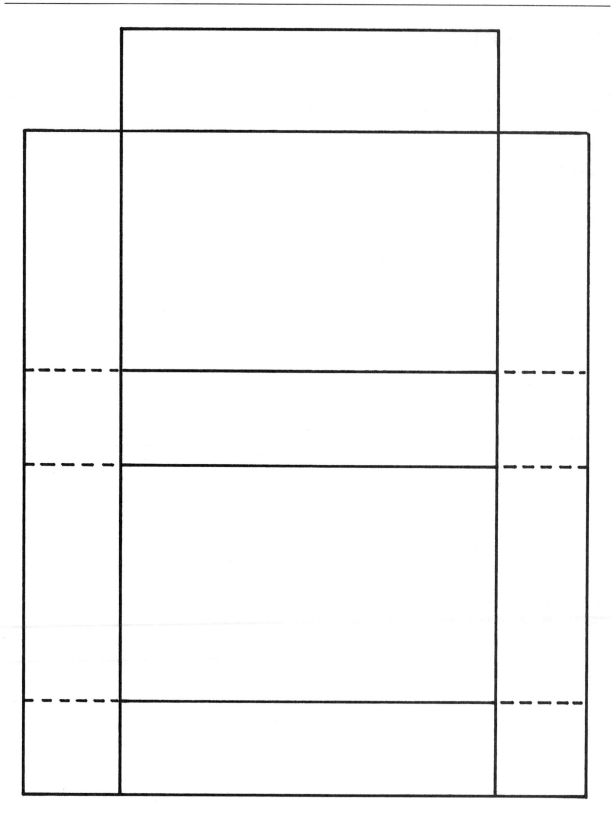

Fig. 4.18. Cereal package activity.

SHOPPING BAGS

The shopping bag that provides customers with a container for carrying their purchases also advertises the name of the store where the merchandise was purchased.

Shopping Bag Design

Design a shopping bag for a local store. Use the pattern in figure 4.19 to construct the bag.

Points to Remember

1. Include the name of the store on the shopping bag.

Supplies

☐ Photocopy of figure 4.19

☐ Drawing and writing tools

☐ Practice paper

Instructions

Select the name of the store. Use the practice paper to make some rough sketches of the bag design. Transfer the final design to the photocopy of figure 4.19. Cut out along the outlines of figure 4.19, then fold and glue form to make the bag.

Science Lesson

Design a shopping bag for a store that specializes in recycled products. Use the pattern in figure 4.19 and newspaper to construct the bag.

Fig. 4.19. Shopping bag activity.

TABLOIDS

Tabloids are a type of magazine that use eye-catching headlines to attract a reader's attention.

Tabloid Cover

Design a tabloid cover.

Points to Remember

1. Exaggerate headlines to attract a reader's attention.

Supplies

☐ Photocopy of figure 4.20

☐ Practice paper

☐ Writing tools

☐ Old magazines

☐ Scissors

☐ Glue

Instructions

Look through old magazines and select two pictures that would not typically be associated with one another, such as a dog's head and a human body. Cut out the two images and glue them together on a photocopy of figure 4.20. Use the information in the picture you created to write copy for a tabloid cover. Write a list of ideas on the practice paper, then organize the ideas into a rough draft. Proofread and revise the draft, then transfer the completed copy to the paper with your unusual image.

History Lesson

Collect as much information as possible about a past public figure. Use some of the facts about this person to make an exaggerated, eye-catching tabloid cover.

Fig. 4.20. Tabloid cover activity.

TRADING CARDS

Trading cards are a type of advertisement that provides information about individual members of sports teams. The cards are not designed to sell a product, but work as a sort of "reminder advertising" that attempts to build a positive image for the player or team and to keep the sport and the athlete in the public eye.

Sports Trading Card

Design a trading card for a popular sports figure.

Points to Remember

1. Use as many sources as possible to locate information about the athlete.

Supplies

☐ Photocopy of figure 4.21

☐ Practice paper

☐ Drawing and writing tools

Instructions

Use the practice paper to collect information about the sports figure selected. Write a rough draft of the information. Proofread and revise the copy, then transfer the information to the back of a photocopied card from figure 4.21. Use an actual set of trading cards for ideas. Draw the person or place a picture of the athlete, from a newspaper or magazine, on the front of the photocopied card.

Geography Lesson

Design a trading card for a city, state, or country.

Science Lesson

Design a trading card for a plant or animal.

Fig. 4.21. Sports trading card activity.

Chapter 5

Advertising Terms

Chapter 5 contains lessons that explore advertising terms. Products and services from many aspects of the students' daily lives are used as topics for advertising writing. The lessons are designed for different levels of involvement: some are as simple as creating a brief headline, others require more in-depth writing. The lessons are organized alphabetically by advertising terms. Suggestions for integrating the lessons are also provided.

ADVOCACY ADVERTISING

Advocacy advertising is a type of institutional advertising that promotes ideas or positions on newsworthy issues. In advocacy advertising, organizations can express their views through the use of media such as posters.

Environmental Poster

Design a poster for an environmental cause.

Points to Remember

1. Use bold letters for the key words.

2. Include a picture on the poster.

Supplies

☐ Any size of paper

☐ Writing and drawing tools

☐ Practice paper

Instructions

Begin by selecting an environmental issue. On the practice paper, write down all of the key words to use on the poster, and make a sketch of the art work. Organize the words and pictures into a rough draft. Proofread and revise the rough draft and sketch, then transfer the completed copy and picture to the final paper.

Politics Lesson

Construct a poster on the subject of a current political issue. Use the front page of the newspaper as an information source.

History Lesson

Throughout history, individuals have taken positions on many political issues. Research past issues and make a poster that expresses the views of people during a particular time in history.

Sample environmental poster.

BAIT AND SWITCH

Bait and switch is an example of deceptive advertising. In bait and switch, a store advertises incredibly low prices to attract customers. However, the retailer does not carry the advertised merchandise; instead, customers are pressured to purchase more expensive products.

Watch Advertisement

Write copy for a newspaper advertisement selling a watch. Make the price very attractive so that it is difficult for the reader to resist coming to the store to make a purchase. Remember, the dishonest intention is to sell a higher priced item once the customer is in the store.

Points to Remember

1. To attract customers, use large letters and include the incredible price in the headline.

2. Make the price considerably lower than real prices of watches.

Supplies

☐ Practice paper

☐ Photocopy of figure 5.1

☐ Writing tools

Instructions

Generate a list of ideas about the advertisement on the practice paper. Organize the ideas into a rough draft. Proofread and revise the draft, then transfer the information to the photocopy of figure 5.1.

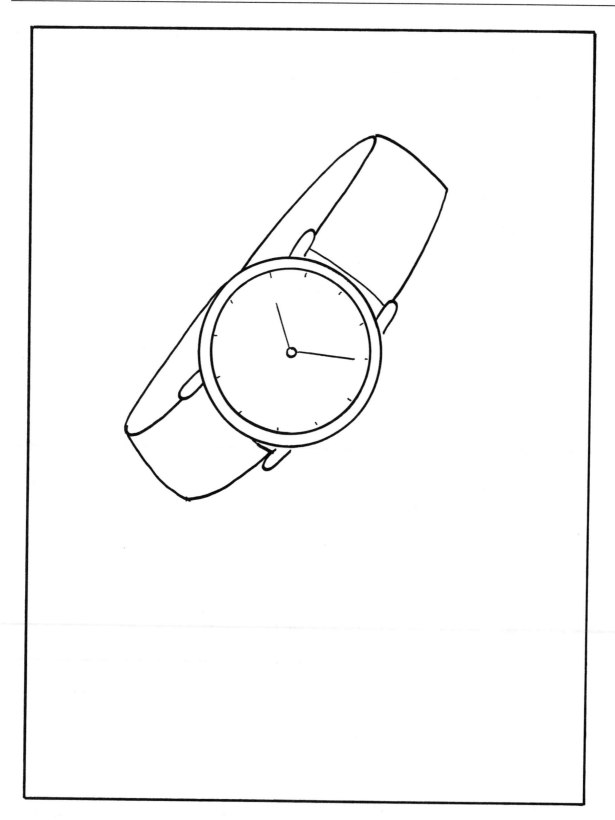

Fig. 5.1. Watch advertisement activity.

BLURB

A book jacket often contains a brief piece of copy that provides information about the contents and quality of the book. This copy is referred to as a blurb.

Book Jacket Blurb

Design a jacket and write a blurb for a book.

Points to Remember

1. Include the title of the book, the name of the author, and an eye-catching illustration on the cover.

2. Write as many positive points as possible to encourage others to read the book.

Supplies

☐ Drawing and writing tools

☐ Practice paper

☐ Book

☐ Paper that fits around the book

Instructions

Use the practice paper to create a list of the book's good points. Make a rough draft of the blurb and the other items to include on the cover. Proofread and revise the rough draft, then transfer the information to a sheet of paper that fits around the book, as shown in the example in figure 5.2.

Literature Lesson

Find a book that contains a blurb on the jacket. Write a new blurb for the book.

Fig. 5.2. Book jacket.

BRAND ADVERTISING

Companies name their products to give them an identity and to help distinguish their products from competitors. A label that includes the product's name sets it apart from other brands that are packaged in the same type of containers. Imagine how difficult it would be to purchase a specific brand of cola or juice if the label was removed.

Beverage Can Label

Use the photocopy of the beverage can label to design a brand of beverage.

Points to Remember

1. Have the label entirely wrap around the can.

Supplies

☐ Photocopy of figure 5.3

☐ Practice paper

☐ Drawing and writing tools

☐ Beverage can

Instructions

Examine many different types of canned beverages. Write a list of the information to include on the label. Make a rough draft of the copy and art work. Proofread and revise the rough draft, then transfer the information from the practice paper to the photocopy of figure 5.3. When completed, cut out the label and attach it with tape or glue to the can.

Fig. 5.3. Beverage can label activity.

BUNDLE

A bundle is the practice of advertising a smaller product along with a larger product. An example: a customer receives 20 gallons of gasoline free or at a discounted price with the purchase of a car.

Newspaper Pizza Advertisement

Design a newspaper advertisement that advertises a large pizza as the main item in a bundle. Select a smaller item to include in the advertisement to make the offer more attractive.

Points to Remember

1. The smaller item should make the main product look more attractive.

Supplies

☐ Practice paper

☐ Drawing and writing tools

☐ Photocopy of figure 5.4

Instructions

Write a list of ideas for the bundle on the practice paper. Select a product to advertise along with the pizza, and make a rough draft of the copy and art work. Proofread and revise the draft, then transfer the information to the photocopy of figure 5.4.

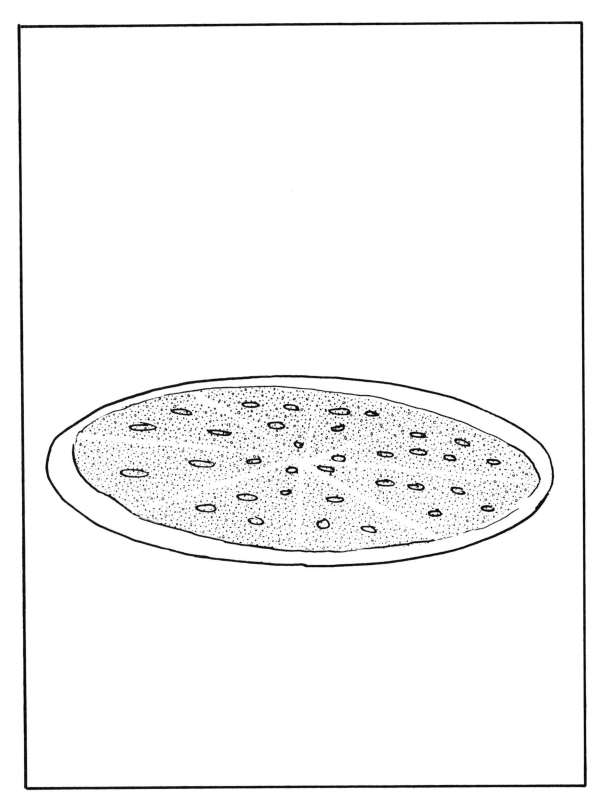

Fig. 5.4. Newspaper pizza advertisement activity.

CHARACTERISTICS

A product's characteristics are descriptions of its qualities.

Newspaper Jeans Advertisement

Use synonyms to write a headline for the jeans in figure 5.5.

Points to Remember

1. A synonym is a word that means the same as another word.

Supplies

☐ Practice paper

☐ Writing tools

☐ Photocopy of figure 5.5

Instructions

Select a word that describes the jeans. Create a list of synonyms for the word. Use the synonyms to write the headline and body copy for the advertisement. Proofread and revise the headline and copy, then transfer them to the photocopy of figure 5.5.

Grammar Lesson

Write a simile for the advertisement. Similes include the words *as* and *like*. For example, the jeans fit like a glove; the jeans are as snug as . . .

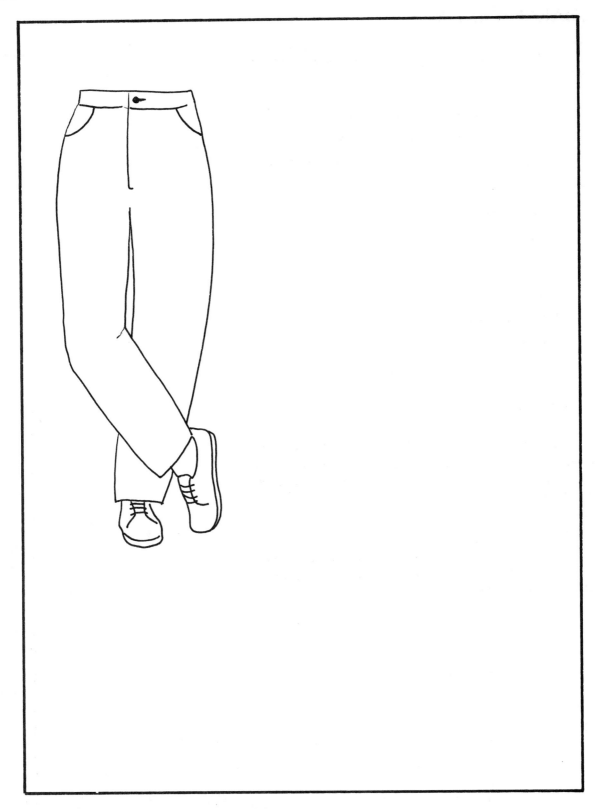

Fig. 5.5. Newspaper jeans advertisement activity.

COMMUNICATION

Communication is providing information about your product or service to potential customers. The information is presented in a way that persuades people to buy. The four main steps to achieving successful communication are to: get the viewer's attention, hold their interest, arouse their desire for the product, and make them act.

Travel Poster

Using the four steps of communication, design a travel poster for a city or state.

Points to Remember

1. Include a drawing or photograph of an appealing aspect of the city or state.

2. Display the name of the city or state in large, bold letters.

Supplies

☐ Writing and drawing tools

☐ Any size of paper

☐ Local or regional newspaper or magazine, if a photograph is needed (optional)

☐ Scissors and glue (optional)

☐ Practice paper

Instructions

Evaluate the city or state to determine the aspects that would attract tourists. List the key points on the practice paper. Sketch a drawing or select a photograph. Construct a rough draft of the poster's copy. Proofread and revise the draft, then transfer the copy and art to a final paper of any size.

Geography Lesson

Research a city, state, or country. Using the facts, design a poster.

Sample travel poster.

COMPARATIVE ADVERTISING

Comparative advertising involves taking two or more products of the same class or group and comparing them in respect to their characteristics.

Magazine Advertisement for Athletic Shoes

Write an advertisement for a particular brand of athletic shoes. Compare it to a similar brand currently on the market. Use antonyms when writing the advertisement.

Points to Remember

1. An antonym is a word that is opposite in meaning to another word.

Supplies

☐ Practice paper

☐ Writing tools

☐ Photocopy of figure 5.6

Instructions

List all of the positive points about the shoes. Then write a second list of the antonyms for each positive point on the first list. Use the lists to create a rough draft of the advertising copy. Proofread and revise the draft, then transfer the information to the photocopy of figure 5.6.

Fig. 5.6. Athletic shoe activity.

CUSTOMER APPRECIATION

Customers need to know that their business is appreciated. An incentive card is a method of thanking customers for their continued business. As stated on the card, after a specified number of purchases, a free item is provided.

Sandwich Shop Incentive Card

Show the customers at a sandwich shop appreciation for their business. Design a card that will earn free food with the purchase of a specific number of items.

Points to Remember

1. Include the store name, location, and business hours.

Supplies

☐ Drawing and writing tools

☐ Practice paper

☐ Photocopy of figure 5.7

Instructions

Write a list on the practice paper of all of the information to include on the incentive card. Organize the information into a rough draft, then proofread and revise the draft. Use one of the blank cards in figure 5.7 for practice and the other for the final card.

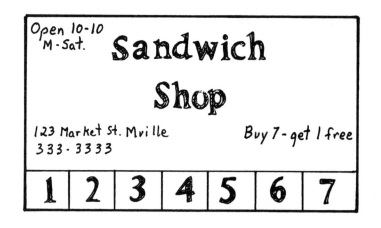

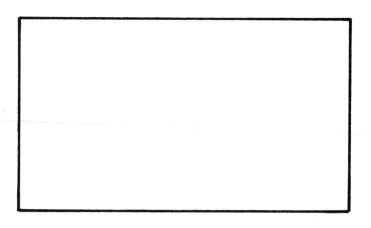

Fig. 5.7. Incentive card activity.

DIRECT RESPONSE

Direct response advertising provides potential customers with information concerning a product or service, as well as a simple method for responding to the advertisement. The major idea behind direct response advertising is convenience.

Book Club Postcard

Design a postcard for the direct response book club advertisement in figure 5.8.

Points to Remember

1. Design the postcard so that it is easy for the customer to complete.

Supplies

☐ Photocopy of figure 5.8

☐ Writing tools

☐ Practice paper

Instructions

Write a list on the practice paper of the information to include on the advertisement and the postcard. Brainstorm titles for the books to be depicted in the illustration. Organize the information into a rough draft. Proofread and revise the draft, then transfer the information to the photocopy in figure 5.8.

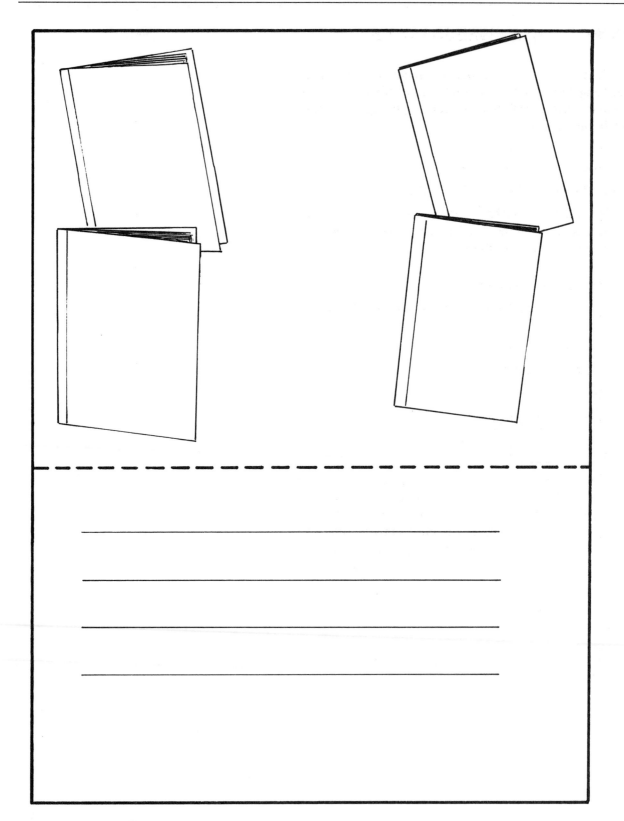

Fig. 5.8. Book club activity.

DIRECT MAIL SWEEPSTAKES

A direct mail sweepstakes is a method of advertising that companies use to increase their visibility. In this type of sweepstakes, customers participate in a game or drawing through the mail.

Sweepstakes Envelope Design

Write an eye-catching headline for the sweepstakes envelope in figure 5.9. The main goal is to persuade the viewer to open the envelope.

Points to Remember

1. Use a headline that attracts a customer's attention.

Supplies

☐ Drawing and writing tools

☐ Practice paper

☐ Photocopy of figure 5.9

Instructions

List a few attention-grabbing statements on the practice paper. Make a rough draft of the copy. A drawing can be added, if desired. Proofread and revise the draft, then transfer the information to the photocopy of figure 5.9. Cut, fold, and glue the paper to form an envelope.

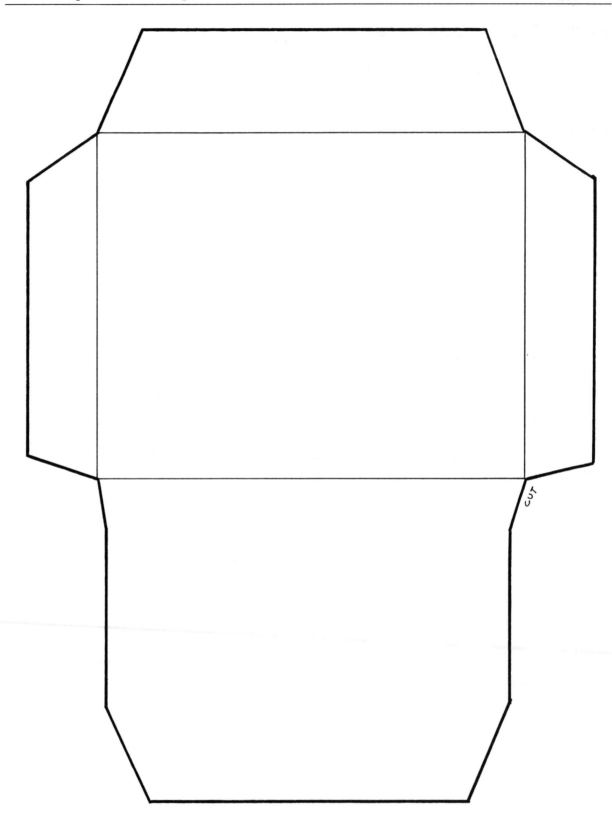

Fig. 5.9. Sweepstakes envelope activity.

GENERIC BRAND

Generic brands are products that are sold in plain, undecorated packages.

Generic Soap Box

Design a box for a generic brand of soap.

Points to Remember

1. Use as little color as possible on the box.

2. Exclude illustrations from the box.

Supplies

☐ Photocopy of figure 5.10

☐ Practice paper

☐ Drawing and writing tools

Instructions

Examine different brand name soap boxes. On the practice paper, write down only the most basic information that is required on the package. After selecting the essential information, make a rough draft of the design. Proofread and revise the design, then transfer it to the photocopy of figure 5.10.

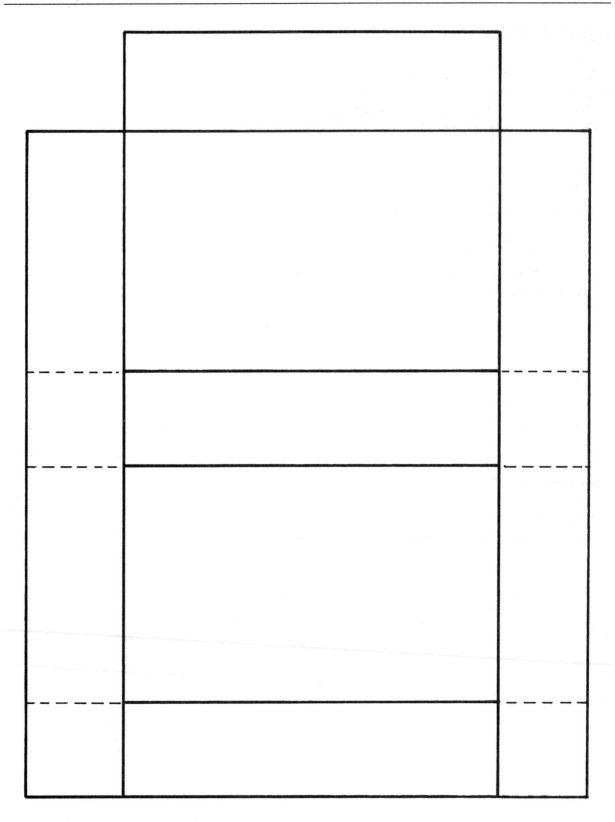

Fig. 5.10. Generic soap box activity.

GROUP PACKAGE

Companies may call attention to their products by using a group package. For this promotion, the products are packaged in a group and offered at a special price— for instance, *buy two get one free* (fig. 5.11).

Sock Package

Construct a group package of socks.

Points to Remember

1. Make the package price bold, so that it attracts attention.

Supplies

☐ Drawing and writing tools

☐ Photocopy of figure 5.12

☐ Practice paper

☐ Construction paper

☐ Scissors

☐ Glue

Instructions

Cut out the sock shape and label from the photocopy in figure 5.12 to use as a guide. Trace and cut out several sock shapes. Use the practice paper to write a list of the information to include on the package. Proofread and revise the copy, then transfer the copy to the package. Fold and attach the package to the top of the socks, as shown in figure 5.11.

Fig. 5.11. Group package label.

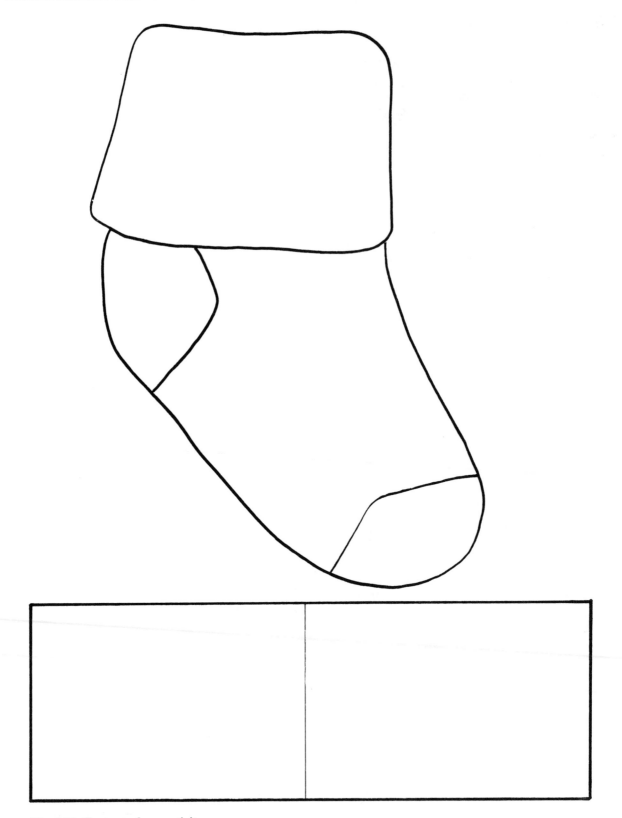

Fig. 5.12. Group package activity.

IMPULSE BUYING

Impulse buying can be described as a "spur of the moment" purchase. Check-out counters in stores and restaurants are areas where products that attract impulse buyers are placed.

Chewing Gum Package

Design a chewing gum package.

Points to Remember

1. Because the package is placed on a display rack with many other brands of gum, it must be designed to stand apart from the rest of the packages.

Supplies

☐ Photocopy of figure 5.13

☐ Writing and drawing tools

☐ Practice paper

Instructions

Examine packages of chewing gum, and choose the important elements. On the practice paper, write down the points to include on the package and make a sketch of the design. Proofread and revise the design, then transfer the information to the photocopy of figure 5.13. Cut, fold, and glue the paper to form the package.

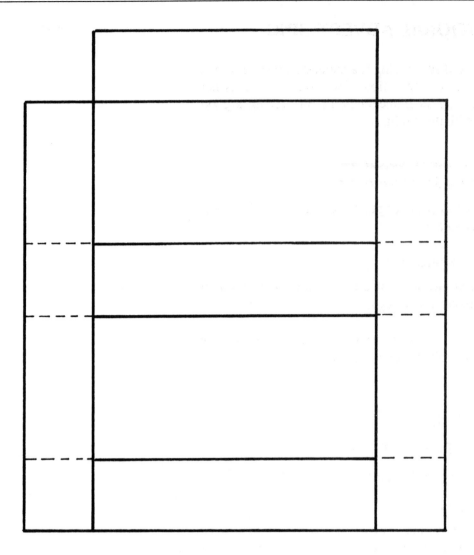

Fig. 5.13. Chewing gum package activity.

INSTITUTIONAL ADVERTISING

Institutional advertising is a method companies use to build an image or reputation. The advertisement is not aimed at making an immediate sale, but rather, a good impression with the public.

Telephone Advertisement

Design a full-page magazine advertisement for a telephone company.

Points to Remember

1. Make the name of the company large, so that it attracts attention.

2. Write the body copy so that it says positive things about the company.

Supplies

☐ Practice paper

☐ Photocopy of figure 5.14

☐ Drawing and writing tools

Instructions

Make a list of the company's positive points on the practice paper. Create a rough draft of the advertisement's headline and body copy. Proofread and revise the copy, then transfer the completed information to the photocopy of figure 5.14.

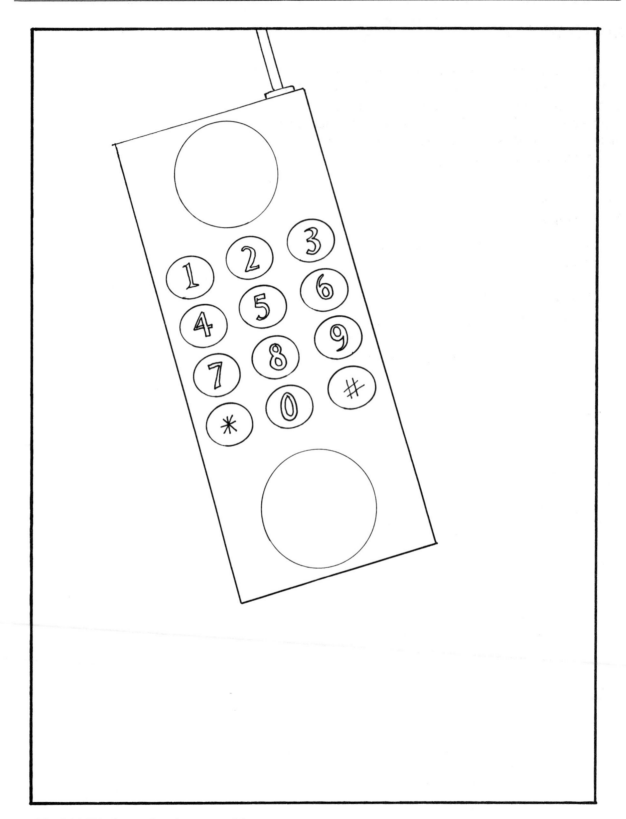

Fig. 5.14. Telephone advertisement activity.

LOGO DESIGN

Many companies use a symbol that people remember and associate with their product or service. This is called a logo. The logo may consist of letters, pictures, or a combination of the two. The shapes of the letters and pictures are usually simplified, which makes them easy to remember. (See fig. 5.15.)

Design a Logo

Using the letters provided in figure 5.16, design a logo.

Points to Remember

1. Keep the design of the logo simple.

2. A logo may be used to give a company character.

Supplies

☐ Photocopy of figure 5.16

☐ Paper

☐ Drawing and writing tools

Instructions

Make a photocopy of figure 5.16. Select the letter to use in the logo. Pressing the photocopied image over a window, trace the letter onto another sheet of paper. Combine the letter with a simple drawing to create a logo.

Math Lesson

Think of all of the different words that are represented by symbols in math: plus (+), minus (-), dollars ($), and equal (=). Design a math logo using initials and a math symbol.

World History Lesson

Ancient Egyptians used hieroglyphics as their written language. Hieroglyphics are a type of writing that uses symbols in place of letters. Create new symbols.

Fig. 5.15. Sample logos.

A B C D E
F G H I J K
L M N O P
Q R S T U
V W X Y Z

Fig. 5.16. Logo letters activity.

LOOK-ALIKES

Notes

Look-alikes are packages that are designed to look similar to a big-selling, well-known product.

Soup Label

Design a label for a brand of soup. Make the label look as similar as possible to a popular brand without making it an exact copy.

Points to Remember

1. Use the same color scheme and similar style type as the name brand product.

Supplies

☐ Photocopy of figure 5.17

☐ Drawing and writing tools

☐ Practice paper

Instructions

Look carefully at the product that will be imitated. Choose the key elements to use in the design. Use the practice paper to make a sketch of the design. Proofread and revise the sketch, then make a final drawing on the photocopy of figure 5.17.

Fig. 5.17. Soup label activity.

PIONEERING ADVERTISING

Pioneering advertising is a method of advertising that promotes a group or a category of products, rather than a specific brand.

Milk Advertisement

Write the copy for the milk advertisement in figure 5.18.

Points to Remember

1. The brand name of the product is not to be used in the advertisement.

Supplies

☐ Practice paper

☐ Drawing and writing tools

☐ Photocopy of figure 5.18

Instructions

Make a list of the product's positive points. Create a rough draft of the headline and body copy. Proofread and revise the copy, then transfer the information to the photocopy of figure 5.18.

Math Lesson

Design an advertisement that promotes the subject of math.

Fig. 5.18. Milk advertisement activity.

REMINDER ADVERTISING

Specialty items are a type of reminder advertising. Items such as pens, notepads, hats, and calculators are imprinted with important information designed to keep a company's name in the public eye.

Hat Advertisement

A product containing a reminder advertisement, such as a hat, is an item that a customer would probably use on a regular basis. The product's owner and others would be reminded of the company advertised on the item. Design a patch for the front of a hat.

Points to Remember

1.   Include the company name, address, phone number, and logo on the patch.

Supplies

☐ Drawing and writing tools

☐ Paper

☐ Practice paper

Instructions

List the information to be included on the patch on the practice paper. Create a rough draft. Proofread and revise the rough draft, then transfer the information to another sheet of paper.

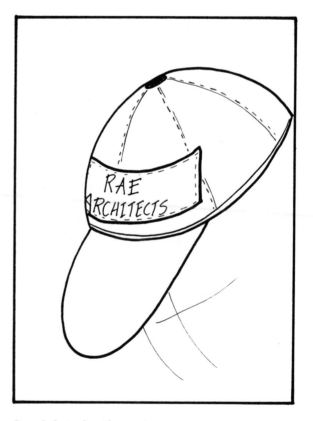

Sample hat advertisement.

SLOGAN

A slogan is a memorable or catchy saying about a product that works to keep it in the consumer's mind. A slogan is a method of reminder advertising.

School Bumper Sticker Slogan

Write a slogan for the school that will appear on a bumper sticker. Bumper stickers are made on paper with an adhesive coating on the back, so that they can be attached to the bumper of a car.

Points to Remember

1. Keep the slogan short.

2. Use rhymes on the bumper sticker, as they are easy to remember.

Supplies

☐ Writing tools

☐ Photocopy of figure 5.19

☐ Practice paper

Instructions

Use the practice paper to write ideas for the slogan. Create a rough draft of the slogan. Proofread and revise the rough draft, then transfer the information to the photocopy of figure 5.19.

Politics Lesson

The motto or slogan for the United States is *e pluribus unum*, which means "out of many, one," or that we are one nation made up of many states. This motto can be found on the one dollar bill. Write a new motto to describe the United States.

History Lesson

Write a slogan to appear on a bumper sticker for a past political election.

Fig. 5.19. Bumper sticker activity.

SOFT ADVERTISING

Soft advertising sets a quiet, peaceful, warm, and loving mood to advertise a product.

Pet Store Advertisement

Design a soft magazine advertisement for a pet store.

Points to Remember

1. Color is one method of setting a peaceful mood.

Supplies

☐ Photocopy of figure 5.20

☐ Old magazines

☐ Scissors

☐ Glue

Instructions

Look through old magazines to find a picture that would give the advertisement in figure 5.20 a soft look.

Family
Pet Store

Fig. 5.20. Pet store advertising activity.

SPECIAL PRICING

Special pricing is the use of a package displaying a boldly printed discounted price to attract attention.

Label Design

Using an empty box from any product and a photocopy of the label design (in figure 5.21), make a new, discounted price label. With the product's original price in mind, determine an attractive, new price.

Points to Remember

1. Use bold letters and colors for the label.

Supplies

☐ An empty product box

☐ Photocopy of figure 5.21

☐ Practice paper

☐ Scissors

☐ Writing and drawing tools

☐ Glue

Instructions

Begin by making a rough draft of the information to include on the label. Proofread and revise the design, then transfer the information from the practice paper to the photocopy of figure 5.21. Cut out and glue the label to the box.

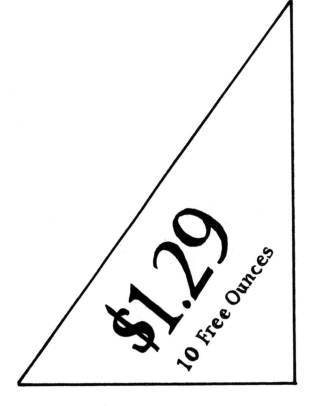

Sample label design.

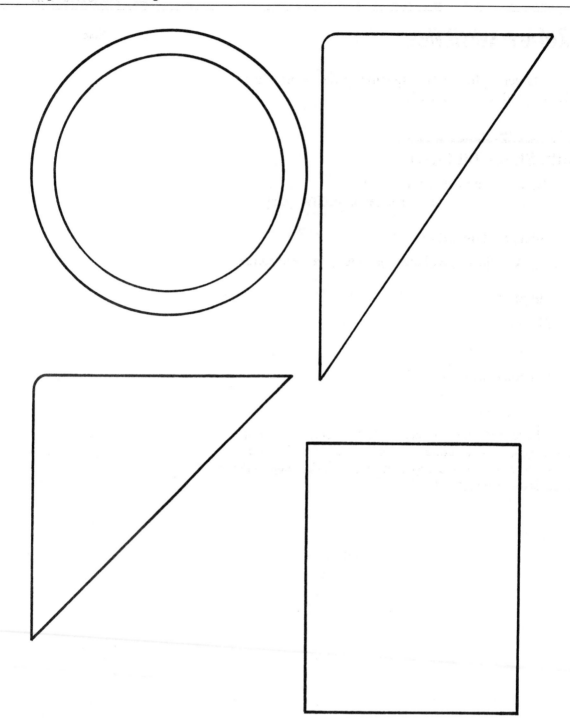

Fig. 5.21. Label design activity.

TARGET AUDIENCE

Notes

A target audience is a specific group of people to which a product is marketed.

Milk Shake Billboard

Use words in the headline and body copy of the milk shake advertisement to speak to a specific group.

Points to Remember

1. Use the name of the target group in the headline.

Supplies

☐ Writing tools

☐ Practice paper

☐ Photocopy of figure 5.22

Instructions

Choose the group to target. Write a rough draft of the advertisement's headline and body copy. Proofread and revise the headline and copy, then transfer the copy to the photocopy of figure 5.22.

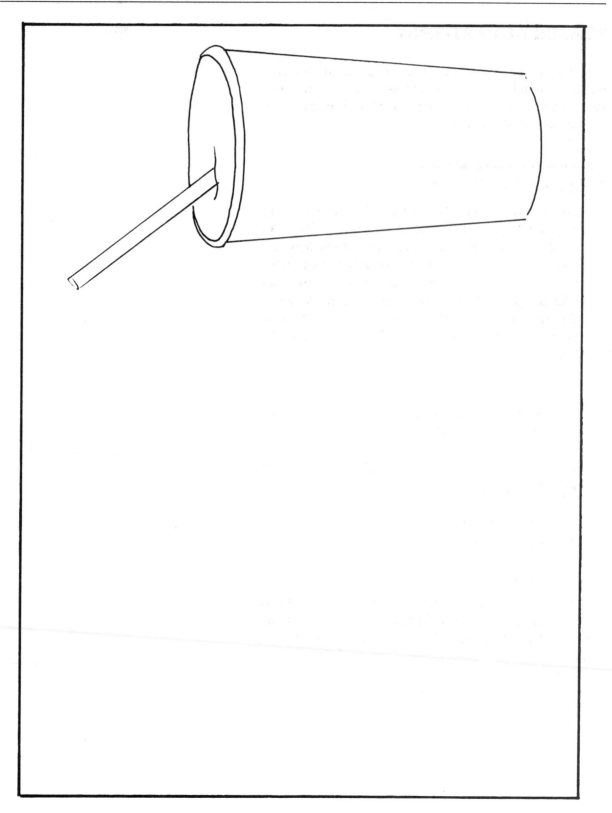

Fig. 5.22. Milk shake billboard activity.

TEASER ADVERTISING

Teaser advertisements are designed to attract a reader's attention by leaving out a portion of the message, such as the product's name or appearance. This leaves the viewer anxious to see more.

Crayon Advertisement

Design a magazine advertisement for a new color of crayon using the technique of teaser advertising. To build a reader's interest in the advertisement, leave the color of the crayon blank and write copy that makes the viewer curious about what the new color looks like. Suggest that the viewer take a specific action to discover the new color, such as buying a pack of crayons, waiting to see next week's ad, or sending for a free crayon.

Points to Remember

1. Attract the viewer's attention to the advertisement with a picture.

Supplies

☐ Writing tools

☐ Photocopy of figure 5.23

☐ Practice paper

Instructions

Using the practice paper, list the information to include on the advertisement. Organize the information into a rough draft. Proofread and revise the draft, then transfer the information to the photocopy of figure 5.23.

Fig. 5.23. Crayon advertisement activity.

TESTIMONIAL

A testimonial is the use of a famous person to promote a product or service.

Juice Advertisement

Select a picture from a magazine of a famous person to use in the juice advertisement in figure 5.24. Write a headline and body copy using statements promoting the product.

Points to Remember

1. Use a celebrity in the advertisement who is famous enough to be recognized by the viewers.

Supplies

☐ Practice paper

☐ Old magazines

☐ Scissors

☐ Writing and drawing tools

☐ Photocopy of figure 5.24

Instructions

Find and cut out a picture of a famous person from an old magazine. Use the practice paper to write ideas for the headline and body copy. Create a rough draft. Proofread and revise the draft, then transfer the completed copy to the photocopy of figure 5.24. Glue the magazine picture to the photocopy.

Literature Lesson

Select a character from a nursery rhyme to promote a product.

History Lesson

Use a famous person from the past to promote a product, service, or company.

Science

Select a famous scientist and design an advertisement that endorses his or her discovery.

Fig. 5.24. Juice advertisement activity.

TRADEMARK

A trademark is a logo, word, slogan, or image that represents a company's product or service. The company has the exclusive legal right to use the trademark. Copyright is another form of legal protection ensuring an individual or company's exclusive right to use a particular logo, work of art, or musical composition.

Menu Design

Many restaurants have special themes that they use as their trademark. The theme may be used in the restaurant's decorations, the clothing the food servers wear, and even the menu. Design a menu using a theme. (See fig. 5.25 for an example.)

Points to Remember

1. Keep the word or picture for the trademark simple.

Supplies

☐ Paper

☐ Drawing and writing tools

☐ Practice paper

Instructions

Use the practice paper to make a list of ideas. Organize the ideas into a rough draft. Proofread and revise the draft, then transfer the completed information to a folded paper.

History Lesson

One of the earliest trademarks was the coat of arms. Design a coat of arms.

Mythology Lesson

Design a trademark for a god or goddess.

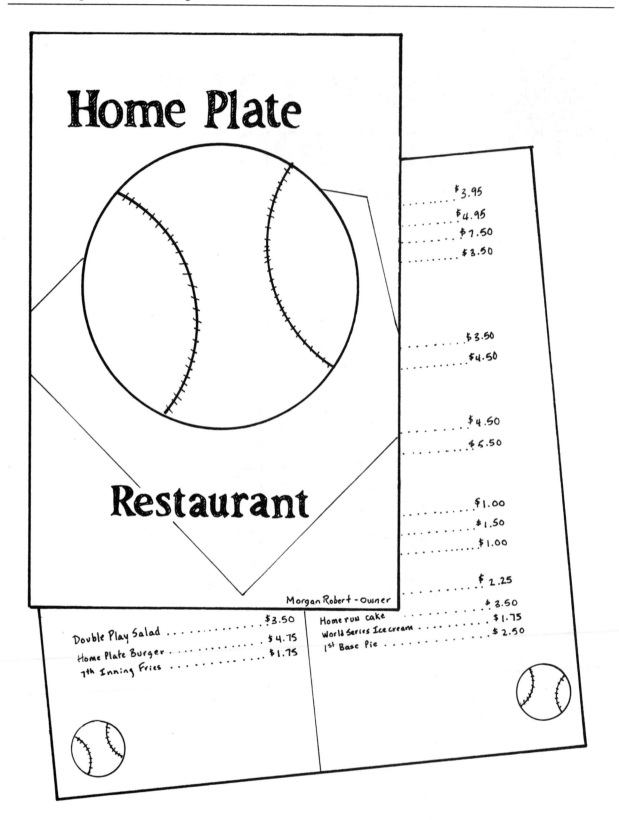

Fig. 5.25. Sample menu design.

ABOUT THE AUTHOR

Photograph by Silver Image

Debi Englebaugh received her Bachelor of Fine Arts degree in drawing from Pennsylvania State University. She later received certification in art education and a Master of Arts in fibers from Edinboro University of Pennsylvania. She has ten years of art education teaching experience, at all grade levels in public and private schools. Debi is also a studio artist and currently works in a variety of areas that include bookbinding, drawing, and photography. Debi lives in Hermitage, Pennsylvania, with her husband, Robert, and two sons, Taylor and Morgan.

From *Teacher Ideas Press*

ART THROUGH CHILDREN'S LITERATURE:
Creative Art Lessons for Caldecott Books
Debi Englebaugh

Help students create art with qualities similar to the award-winning illustrations of 57 Caldecott books. Myriad lessons focus on such principles and elements as line, color, texture, shape, value, and space. Each has step-by-step instructions, a materials list, and detailed illustrations. **Grades K–6.**
xii, 199p. 8½x11 paper ISBN 1-56308-154-7

ART PROJECTS MADE EASY: Recipes for Fun
Linda J. Arons

Fun, quick, and easy as pie, these art lessons provide an entire year of art activities! Using a variety of media, students explore art principles, collage, crafts, drawing, painting, holiday and seasonal art, multicultural art, and curriculum connections. **Grades 1–6.**
xv, 165p. paper ISBN 1-56308-342-6

GLUES, BREWS, AND GOOS:
Recipes and Formulas for Almost Any Classroom Project
Diana F. Marks

Pulling together hundreds of practical, easy recipes and formulas for classroom projects—from paints and salt map mixtures to volcanic action compounds—these kid-tested projects make learning authentic and enjoyable. All projects use ingredients that are easy to find and processes that are up-to-date. Tips on when, why, and how to use these terrific concoctions are also included. **Grades K–6.**
xvi, 179p. 8½x11 paper ISBN 1-56308-362-0

SUPER KIDS PUBLISHING COMPANY
Debbie Robertson and Patricia Barry

This is it—a complete guide to writing! From planning, drafting, revising, editing, illustrating, printing, and binding to sharing published works with classmates, teachers, and parents, the authors describe how centers can accommodate every step of the writing process.
Grades 3–8.
xiii, 354p. 8½x11 paper ISBN 0-87287-704-3

ARTSTARTS: Drama, Music, Movement, Puppetry, and Storytelling Activities
Martha Brady and Patsy T. Gleason

Selected as Editor's Choice by *Learning Magazine*, this book makes it easy to integrate the arts into the classroom. Teachers and students alike love its lively integrated approach and classroom-tested activities. **Grades K–6.**
xii, 219p. 8½x11 paper ISBN 1-56308-148-2

EXPLORATIONS IN BACKYARD BIOLOGY:
Drawing on Nature in the Classroom, Grades 4–6
R. Gary Raham

Discover life science adventures in your own backyard (or school yard)! Exciting classroom and field activities give students the opportunity for hands-on exploration. Using drawing and writing skills, they record their experiences in a Naturalist's Notebook, which encourages further discoveries. **Grades 4–6.**
xix, 204p. 8½x11 paper ISBN 1-56308-254-3

For a FREE catalog or to order these or any Teacher Ideas Press titles, please contact:

Teacher Ideas Press
Dept. B29 • P.O. Box 6633 • Englewood, CO 80155-6633
Phone: 1-800-237-6124, ext. 1 • Fax: 303-220-8843 • E-mail: lu-books@lu.com •
Web site: www.lu.com/tip